Gifted Wrapping

Gifted Wrapping

Creative Wraps and Ribbons for Every Occasion

Step-by-Step Instructions for Stylish and
Elegant Gift Wraps for Perfect "Present"ations

Christine Fritsch

GLOUCESTER MASSACHUSETTS

QUARRY BOOKS

First published in the United States of America by
Quarry Books, a member of
Quayside Publishing Group
33 Commercial Street
Gloucester, Massachusetts 01930-5089
Telephone: (978) 282-9590
Fax: (978) 283-2742
www.rockpub.com

Library of Congress Cataloging-in-Publication Data

Fritsch, Christine.
    Gifted wrapping : creative wraps and ribbons for every occasion : step-by-step instructions
for stylish and elegant gift wraps for perfect presentations / Christine Fritsch.
        p.   cm.
    Includes index.
    ISBN 1-59253-241-1 (pbk.)
    1. Gift wrapping. I. Title.
TT870.F74 2006
745.54—dc22   2005025494
                                                                                CIP

ISBN 1-59253-241-1

10 9 8 7 6 5 4 3 2 1

Design: Terry Patton Rhoads
Cover Design: Terry Patton Rhoads
Cover Image and Photography: Allan Penn Photography
Illustrations: Wendy Edelson

- To my mom, a person who has given me so many of life's important gifts, all too special to be wrapped in a pretty box. She taught me to embellish the sentiment.

- To my boys big and small: James, Wyatt, and Owen.

- To all my family who sacrificed their time to make it possible for me to write this book with two toddlers running around me.

Contents

Introduction

In our busy world, people often wait until the last minute to prepare a gift, making them rush through and dread the thought of wrapping it. Another part of the problem is the perfectionist in all of us. We really want to give the perfectly wrapped gift with a big lavish bow, but fearing that we are going to fall short makes us want to throw in the towel—and throw the gift in a gift bag. I want to give people the confidence that they can wrap a beautiful gift. It may not be perfect every time, but the effort you put into it will be truly appreciated by the gift's recipient. Now really—what fun is it to reach into a gift bag? By comparison, there is something almost primal about ripping the paper off a gorgeous gift that turns us all into five-year-old children again.

The gift wrapping you will find in this book is simple and elegant, with an air of sophistication. These techniques are inspired by the Japanese style of gift wrapping and have a real *wow* factor. You will learn the foundations of paper-folding techniques, and I will share tips that professional gift wrappers use to attain a perfect, neat package every time, no matter what the size or shape of the gift. Once you've mastered the basics, the gift wraps in this book should inspire you to build your own style.

There is something about receiving a beautifully wrapped gift that touches the child in all of us.

These wrapping techniques are inspired by the Japanese style of gift wrapping and have a real "wow" factor.

I must confess that I've always loved to wrap gifts. Even at a very young age, the gifts I wrapped and placed under the Christmas tree matched and followed a theme every year. (Little did I realize that "professional gift wrapper" could be a career choice!) After college, I worked in New York City in the children's apparel business, which suited me well as a big part of my job was decorating kid's clothes with ribbons and bows.

After I married, I followed my husband, who was in the Navy, to Japan—a move that filled my life with priceless experiences. I was amazed that I could buy my favorite pastry for a dollar, and that it was wrapped and presented to me with such care and attention to detail. I saved all kinds of wrapping and packing materials from Japan. When I received a gift, I'd carefully remove the paper and study it to figure out precisely how the folds were done. There is an ingenious way of wrapping a package on an angle, using just one piece of tape to seal the whole gift, that is still a mystery to me.

A sophisticated, simply wrapped package is always appropriate and appreciated. An elegant presentation can elevate the value of any gift and says the giver really cares.

After returning to the United States, I was literally walking the streets of New York one day, wondering what to do next, when I found the answer right in front of me at Kate's Paperie. I was drawn into this whimsical store, which has a huge wall of decorative paper visible from the street. I had no idea that gift wrapping could become a profession, that one could get paid to wrap gifts while using the most fantastic assortment of paper and ribbon.

Though business was crazily busy during the holiday season, the job was perfect for a creative person who craved a hands-on outlet. I began teaching classes in Japanese-inspired gift wrapping. While at Kate's, I tried to spread the good word about gift wrapping to all customers: it should be a pleasure, not a chore. The thought and time devoted to the wrapping and presentation should be as important as the gift itself.

A coworker at Kate's nominated me in Scotch Tape's Most-Gifted Wrapper contest. If you're reading this book, then it's definitely a contest you should enter. Every year during the holidays, Scotch Tape sponsors a contest that seeks to crown the nation's most talented wrapper. Entering the contest requires submitting a short essay on what makes you the United States' top wrapper. After the essays are evaluated, four amateurs and four professionals are chosen to come to New York City for a big "wrap off." The contestants are judged on neatness, speed, and creativity through three rounds of competition. In addition to the challenge of the time limit, the odd- and unusual-shaped gifts that are provided to be wrapped add another "dimension" to the task.

Winning the contest has given me more opportunities to do what I love—creative gift wrapping! "It's too pretty to open!" is—and always will be—music to my ears.

For more information on Scotch Tape's Most-Gifted Wrapper contest, visit Scotch's website, www.3m.com.

–Christine Fritsch

Paper and Supplies

The beauty of the art of gift wrap is that the supplies needed are rather basic. Most often, a beautiful wrap can be created using supplies most people have on hand. With a healthy dose of creativity and an abundance of ideas, everyday supplies can be transformed into an elegant presentation.

I have two tips concerning supplies. One is to keep a special container just for your wrapping supplies. Always be on the lookout for special paper and embellishments to add to your stash. It is a wonderful thing to open your container full of supplies and be inspired, each time, by all the goodies you have been collecting.

My second tip concerning supplies pertains to quality: don't be afraid to splurge on special paper and ribbons. Most often, it is easier to wrap with a better-quality paper and ribbon. Higher-quality paper does not rip when wrapping, and it is more forgiving if tape has to be pulled up and moved. A better-quality ribbon will hold its shape much better than inexpensive ribbon, which tends to look a bit worked over by the time you get it into a bow.

However, I am a realist—I do have rolls of inexpensive paper for quick wraps, and I do have fifty-yard (46 m) rolls of inexpensive ribbon. After all, I am a mom first and a professional gift wrapper second!

Wrapping gifts in folded paper is an elegant and ingenious Japanese tradition that can be adapted to nearly any package.

Paper

I would like to stress alternatives to traditional wrapping paper on a roll. There are occasions for paper on a roll, but many times the quality of these papers makes them difficult to work with. There are many affordable handmade and machine-made papers with wonderful textures and patterns. These unique papers can add a style to a wrap that cannot be found in mass-produced paper. There are also many wonderful resources on the Web for handmade paper, and some are listed in the back of the book. In New York, a pilgrimage to Kate's Paperie is a must for experiencing the wonder of handmade paper in person.

Recently, styles of gift wrap and presentation have begun mirroring trends in fashion and home décor. When shopping for supplies, it is common to see the same colors in stationery and gift shops as you see in the glossy magazines and on the clothing racks. Bright pinks and oranges, as well as Victorian palettes of muted grays and purples, have all blossomed in the gift-wrap market. These papers are complemented by shimmering and grosgrain bows, glitter, gemstones, and other sparkly embellishments.

Layering papers and embellishments has become a popular method of personalizing wraps. With so many choices of fabrics and papers, gift-givers are layering semi-translucent fabrics with fun patterns to create new paper combinations. By choosing a trademark gift tag, a lush satin bow, or a palette of vivid colors and using these accents on every gift, gift-wrappers can develop a signature look their friends and loved ones are sure to remember.

1 Marble

2 Lace

3 Unryu

4 Natural Fiber

5 Lace Cut-out

6 Natural Fiber with Straw

7 Leaf Print

8, 9, 10 Marble

11, 12, 14 Embossed

13 Velvet

15 Japanese Washi

Ribbons

Ribbons come in many textures and designs. Here are brief descriptions and some of the pros and cons of the most common ribbons. One thing to remember is that cheap ribbon usually behaves poorly. Often, inexpensive ribbon just doesn't have the body to make a nice bow, or it gets crushed and wrinkled during the bow-making process. If it's a special gift, it is worth it to use a better ribbon. Plus, better ribbon can be saved and reused.

Double-Faced Satin (2, 4, 5)

Double-faced satin is shiny on both sides, and is the best type of satin ribbon to work with.

Grosgrain (7, 9)

Grosgrain ribbon has a ribbed texture. It has a heavy hand and will not produce a big, fluffy bow. However, grosgrain ribbon is a classic material that produces crisp, clean lines. It also comes in many colors and often is printed with a pattern on one side. Once again, be careful with single-sided ribbon, because it is difficult to make a bow with all the "good" sides facing out.

Jacquard (1, 10)

Jacquard ribbon has a detailed design woven into the material. It has a definite right and wrong side.

Metallic (not shown)

Shiny metallic ribbon can be difficult to work with, and woven metallic ribbon tends to pull apart in the middle if the ribbon is worked too hard.

Novelty Ribbon (13–17)

Novelty ribbon is more correctly termed *trim*. There are thousands of fun trims, mostly borrowed from the apparel industry, and they make great embellishments for a wrapped gift.

Satin (not shown)

A very shiny polyester that comes in many vibrant colors and shades, satin ribbon has a heavy, luxurious weight and feel (or hand) but not a lot of body. It will not make a fluffy, bouncy bow. It is best suited for basic bows and is too heavy for multiple-loop bows.

Sheer Ribbon (not shown)

Sheer ribbons are usually inexpensive, and they produce the big, fluffy bows that are most desirable. The drawbacks of sheer ribbon are that it doesn't come in really strong colors and the transparent ribbon can get lost on a busy wrap.

Single-Faced Satin (11, 12)

Single-faced satin has one shiny side and one flat side. It can be more difficult to work with when making bows, because it is hard to manipulate the bow to get all the shiny sides of the ribbon to show.

Tulle (not shown)

Tulle is a sheer, sometimes stiffened, netlike fabric. Tulle now comes in precut rolls and is fun and easy to work with.

Velvet (6, 8)

Velvet ribbon has a plush pile on one side and is usually flat on the other. Velvet is a beautiful, rich-looking ribbon, but because it is heavy and one-sided, it is difficult to use in bow making.

Wire-Edged Jacquard (not shown)

The wire edge helps give this ribbon some body.

Wire-Edged Taffeta (3)

Usually made from synthetic fibers, taffeta has a crisp hand and a bit of shine. Many taffetas come with a wire edge. The wire-edge ribbon is a blessing and a curse. The wire does help a bow hold its shape well, but if the ribbon is worked too much, the wire becomes kinky and the edge looks unattractive.

1

2

3

4

Supplies

Supplies for gift wrapping are basic, and many households have them already, but I would like to stress the use of quality supplies and tools. Better supplies may cost a little more up front, but they will save you hours of frustration in the long run. Keep your wrapping scissors separate from other household scissors, as this will ensure they remain sharp and not be dulled by everyday use. Decorative-edge scissors add fun detailing to the cut edges of paper. Good quality clear tape, both single- and double-sided, such as Scotch brand by 3M, always sticks where it is supposed to, and is forgiving enough to peel back if a mistake is made. (The pop-up tape dispenser is great convenience as it frees up a hand when wrapping.)

1. Transparent ruler

2. Ribbon scissors

3. Bone folder

4. Scissors

5. Single-sided tape

6. Hot glue gun and glue sticks (glue sticks not shown)

7. Pop-up tape dispenser

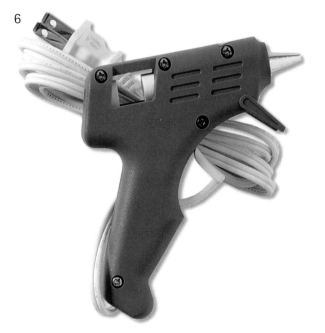

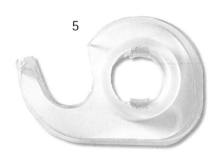

CHAPTER ONE

Paper Wrapping Basics

Even the prettiest paper and most expensive ribbon in the world can be ruined by a messy wrapping job. This chapter will show you the basic techniques of foolproof gift wrapping.

The first topics to be covered will be sizing the paper to the box and folding perfect ends. If these basics are not mastered, the neatness and overall appearance of the package can be compromised. There are a few tricks to ensure the proper fit of paper to box. People often struggle with too little paper or too much, becoming so frustrated just trying to close the ends that they never get to enjoy the fun, creative part of wrapping a gift.

The second part of this chapter will discuss the basic pleating techniques inspired by Japanese gift wrapping. Traditional Japanese gift wrapping is amazingly complicated, and there is a code of gift wrapping. In Japan, it is not just putting paper on a box; much thought goes into to the presentation of a gift. Different colors of paper symbolize happy or sad occasions. The number of pleats created in the paper, and the direction in which they face, also have symbolism. Although the folding techniques in this book are inspired by traditional Japanese gift wrapping, they do not adhere to the Japanese wrapping codes. That could fill another book.

Mastering the basics of fitting and wrapping paper around a package, no matter what its shape, is the first step toward creating polished and professional-looking gifts.

Basic Techniques

"How much paper do I need?" is the number one question asked at Kate's Paperie, a paper and wrapping boutique in New York City. Many gift givers have shorted themselves in the rush to get to a party. Nothing is more frustrating than estimating how much paper is needed to cover the box fully, cutting the paper, and then finding it is too short! A perfect end is neat, but not bulky, and has no tape showing. It sounds simple, but is not that easily achieved.

Properly measuring wrapping paper before cutting ensures perfectly fitted ends and seams.

Sizing Paper to Box

Here is a simple, foolproof way to size the paper properly around the box.

Steps

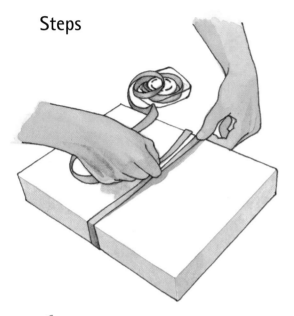

1. Wrap a piece of ribbon or string around the box, and add 2" (5.1 cm) to its length.

2. Lay the ribbon out on the paper and mark its measurement on the back of the paper. This is the length of paper needed to go around the box. Remember that you can always cut away extra, but you can never add more.

materials

ribbon or string

wrapping paper

tools

ruler

pencil

scissors

Side Seams

Use this technique instead of overlapping paper on the back of the box.

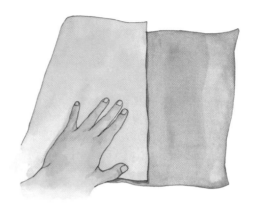

1. Lay the box on the unfinished side of the paper and pull the left side of the paper up and over the entire back of the box until it aligns perfectly with the right edge of the box (facing you).

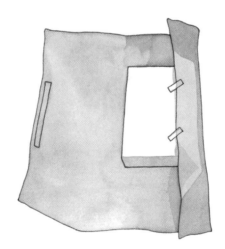

2. Holding the box in place on the paper, release the left edge, and then tape the right side of the paper to the back of the box with single-sided tape. Adhere a long piece of double-sided tape to the wrong side of the left edge of the paper. Then pull the left edge back over the box and adhere to it to the right edge. The seam of paper will disappear at the corner of the box.

materials

wrapping paper

single-sided tape

double-sided tape

tools

bone folder

scissors

Styling Tip

If the raw edge of the paper (the edge that will be visible on the outside of the package) is not cut straight, it can be folded under about ½" (1.3 cm), then aligned with the edge of the package and taped down in place. Use a bone folder for a crisp, even crease.

Rectangular Box Ends

Here's how to make perfect ends on a rectangular box.

A perfect box end lends an elegant finish to a package; it should be evenly folded with no visible tape.

Steps

1. First, size the paper to the box. For a rectangular box, the paper should overhang the ends by a measurement that is the depth of the box plus 1" (2.5 cm). For example, if the box is 1" (2.5 cm) deep, the overhang at both ends should be 2" (5.1 cm).

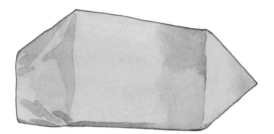

2. Work with the top of the box facedown on the table or work surface. Push one corner of paper in flush to the box, then go to other end and push both corners at the other end flush to the box. Pushing just one corner first, then going to other end will eliminate the problem of the box sliding out of the paper at the opposite end while you are taping the first end.

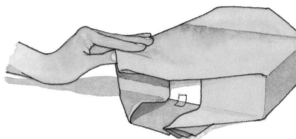

3. The ends must be pushed in all the way, until they are flat and the flaps form perfect right angles at the corners of the box. Failure to get these flat and tight against the box will result in a very sloppy wrap.

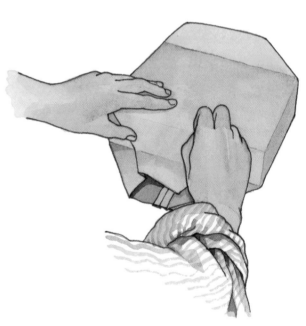

4. Crease the bottom flap in two places: first, as it wraps over the bottom of the box; second, where it meets the top of the box.

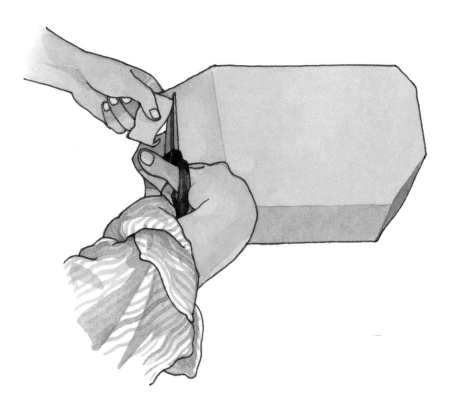

materials

wrapping paper

double-sided tape

tools

scissors

bone folder

5. Cut away excess paper along the second crease. Tape the bottom flap to the box using double-sided clear tape placed beneath the flap.

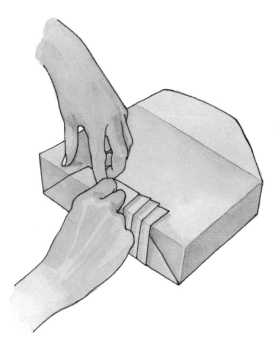

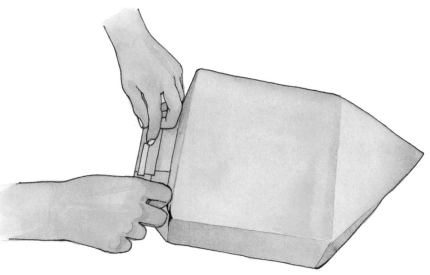

7. When the top flap is folded over, it will be the exact depth of the box. Use double-sided tape at the edge of the flap to secure it in place. After one end is secure, close the other end, following the same steps. No tape should be visible on the closed ends.

6. Bring the top flap over the bottom of the box crease where it meets the bottom edge of the box. Crease it in with the bone folder.

Square Box Ends

Use this technique for making perfect ends on a square box.

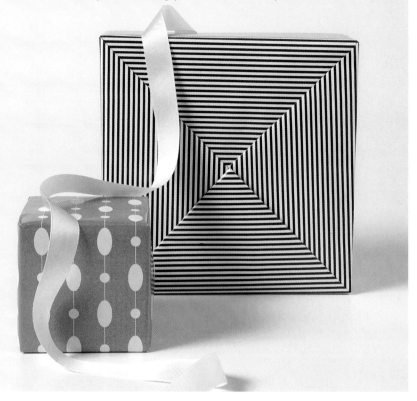

Steps

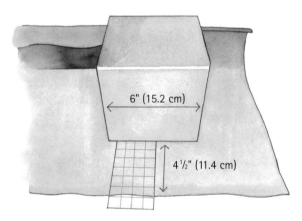

1. Size the paper to the box. To get the points to line up perfectly, measure the end of the box. The overhang at the ends of the box should be three-quarters of the box's depth. For example, if the end measures 6" (15.2 cm), the overhang should be 4½" (11.4 cm).

2. Work with the top of the box facing down on the table. The bottom will be facing up. Push the overhanging paper down over the bottom end of the box. Tape this first flap down with single-sided tape. Then go to work on the other end, also pushing the paper over the bottom of the box first. Pushing just one side first, then going to other end will eliminate the problem of the box sliding out of the paper at the opposite end while you are taping the first end.

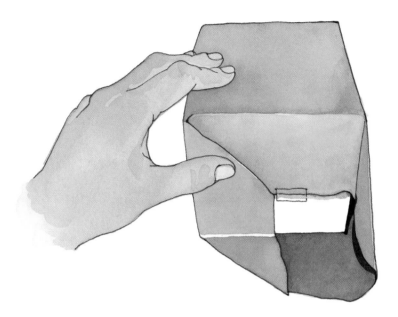

materials

wrapping paper

single-sided tape

double-sided tape

tools

ruler

scissors

bone folder

3. Staying at the same end of the box, push the left side in flat against the box. Use double-sided tape on the underside of the flap to attach it to the box.

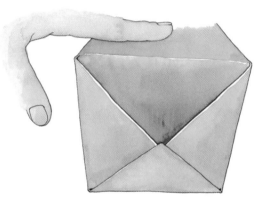

Styling Tip

Using double-sided tape on the under-side of each flap will keep the ends of the paper smooth against the box.

5. Bring up the top flap and crease it in place with the bone folder. Tape it to the box with double-sided tape. Follow the same steps at the other end of the box.

4. Push the right side in flat against the box and use double-sided tape on the under-side of the flap to attach it to the box. When the right and left sides are completely flat against the box, the top flap will form a perfect triangle.

Basic Paper Folding

The following techniques are the building blocks of any gift wrap project. These elements will be used throughout the book. Mastering them will give you innumerable options for all "present"ations!

Three-Pleat Wrap

Simple and sophisticated, this Three-Pleat Wrap is the base for the Japanese-inspired gift wrapping in this book. Once this basic technique is mastered, it can be incorporated into endless combinations of truly spectacular gift wraps.

Basic Techniques

Rectangular Box Ends (page 24)

Getting Started

Size the paper around the box, measuring approximately 1½ times around box to ensure enough paper for the pleats. Once you are comfortable with this technique, you can reduce the amount of paper accordingly.

materials

wrapping paper

single-sided tape

double-sided tape

tools

ruler

scissors

bone folder

Steps

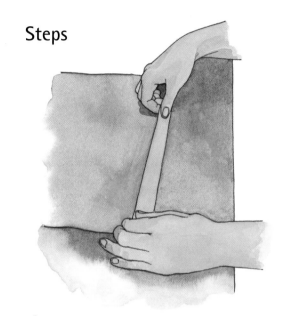

1. Work with the good side of the paper down and the long length of the paper facing away from you. Fold the raw edge up just ½" (1.3 cm) to make a clean edge to start with.

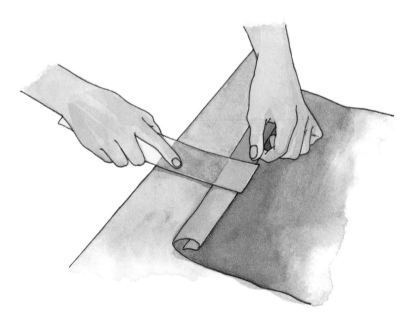

The pleated look of folded wrapping paper has a rich, intricate look, but it is easily mastered. Once mastered, this basic folding technique can be used in any number of wrapping applications.

2. Continue working with the folded edge away from you, and make a second fold 1½" (3.8 cm) wide.

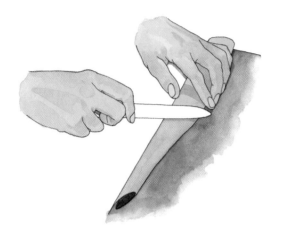

3. Continue folding the right edge, making three equal folds, each measuring 1½" (3.8 cm) wide. Crease the three folds together with the bone folder.

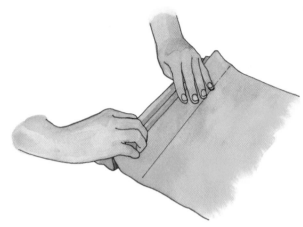

5. Pull the first crease about halfway to the finished edge, creating a ½" (1.3 cm) space between the finished edge and the first crease.

4. Turn the paper over and work with the good side facing up. Unfold all the 1½" (3.8 cm) folds, leaving the first ½" (1.3 cm) fold in place.

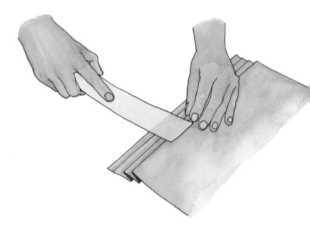

6. Pull the next two folds toward the finished edge in the same manner. All edges should be evenly spaced and about ½" (1.3 cm) apart. When you are finished, there will be four pleats, each ½" (1.3 cm) apart. Crease the pleats into place with the bone folder.

Styling Tip

The pleats need to be very tight on the box or the package will look sloppy. Be generous with the amount of tape on the underside of the pleat.

7. Turn the paper back over to the wrong side and tape the pleats into position using long pieces of single-sided tape on the diagonal. How much tape you need will depend on the length of the pleats. Be generous with the tape holding the pleats in place, and use at least two or three pieces.

9. Once the pleats are properly aligned on the box, hold the box in place on the paper. Without shifting the box, bring the left side up and tape it into place with single-sided tape.

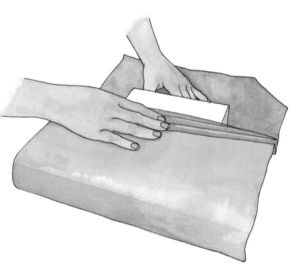

8. Place the box in the center of the paper. The pleats will come up over from the right side. Pull the pleats over the box until they are about one-third of the box's width away from the left side.

10. To secure the pleats to the box, use a long piece of double-sided tape placed about ¼" (6 mm) in from the edge on the underside of the pleats. Wrap the pleats around the box and tape in place with lengths of double-sided tape.

11. Finish the ends of the box just as you would with a plain wrap (see Basics, page 24).

Tuxedo Pleat

The Tuxedo Pleat uses the same folding principles as the Three-Pleat Wrap, but it is a much more formal-looking wrap. With this technique, it is even more important to make straight, even folds. The Tuxedo Pleat is attractive because it leaves a wide center pleat that serves to showcase ribbons and embellishments.

Basic Techniques

Rectangular Box Ends (page 24)

Getting Started

Size the paper around box, measuring approximately 1½ times around box to ensure enough paper for the pleats. Once you are comfortable with this technique, you can reduce the amount of paper accordingly.

Steps

1. Follow steps 1 through 4 of the Three-Pleat Wrap (see page 29).

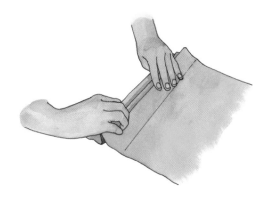

2. Pull the first crease about halfway toward the finished edge, creating a ½" (1.3 cm) space between the finished edge and the first crease.

3. Pull the second crease away from the finished edge and the first crease. Pull it halfway toward the third crease, creating a

½" (1.3 cm) space between the second and third creases, leaving the wide fold intact. The wide space will measure 1½" (3.8 cm), the original measurement of the folds.

4. Pull the third and final crease approximately ½" (1.3 cm) away from the finished edge. After all the pleats are in place, and are straight and even, crease them into place with the bone folder.

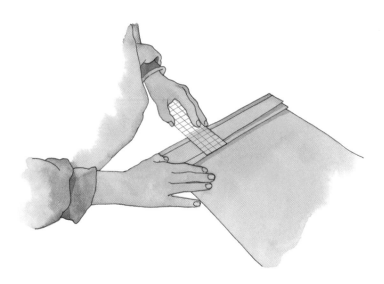

5. Follow steps 7 through 10 of the Three-Pleat Wrap (page 31) to secure the pleats in place and adhere the paper to the box. Finish the ends of the box just as you would with a plain wrap (see Basics, page 24).

materials

wrapping paper

single-sided tape

double-sided tape

tools

ruler

scissors

bone folder

Reverse Tuxedo Pleat

The Reverse Tuxedo Pleat is a slight variation on the standard Tuxedo Pleat.
A simple flip of the paper makes a big impact. If you can find two-sided
paper, the effect will be even more dramatic. This is a great way to dress
up a gift if ribbons and other embellishments are not going to be used.

Basic Techniques

Rectangular Box Ends (page 24)

Getting Started

Size the paper around box, measuring approximately 1½ times around box to ensure enough paper for the pleats. Once you are comfortable with this technique, you can reduce the amount of paper accordingly.

Steps

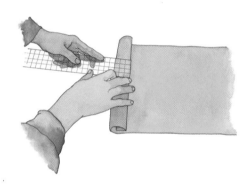

1. Working with the good side of the paper facing up, follow steps 1 through 4 of the Three-Pleat Wrap (page 29). The folds will all be on the wrong side of the paper, facing out.

2. Turn the paper over and work with the wrong side of the paper facing up. Pull the first crease about halfway toward the finished edge, creating a ½" (1.3 cm) space between the finished edge and the first crease.

3. Pull the second crease away from the finished edge and the first crease. Pull it halfway toward the third crease, creating a ½" (1.3 cm) space between the second and third creases, leaving the wide fold intact. The wide space will measure 1½" (3.8 cm), the original measurement of the folds. After all the pleats are in place, straight, and even, crease them with the bone folder.

4. Tape the pleats into place using single-sided tape on the diagonal. Fold the pleats down using the third crease as a guide. Apply double-sided tape to the underside edge to hold it in place. Turn the paper back over so the good side is facing up. Fold solid pleats back over onto printed side of paper.

5. Follow steps 8 through 10 of the Three-Pleat Wrap (page 31) to adhere the paper to the box. Finish the ends of the box as with a plain wrap (see Basics, page 24).

materials

wrapping paper

single-sided tape

double-sided tape

tools

ruler

scissors

bone folder

Fan Pleat

The Fan Pleat follows the same basic idea of the Three-Pleat Wrap, but simply turns the paper on an angle. It is an interesting wrap that can stand on its own without any further embellishment.

Basic Techniques

Rectangular Box Ends (page 24)

Getting Started

Size the paper around box, measuring approximately 1½ times around box to ensure enough paper for the pleats. Once you are comfortable with this technique, you can reduce the amount of paper accordingly. When sizing paper to the ends of the box, a more generous amount of paper is needed to compensate for the loss in height that occurs when the fan is folded in. For example, if the box is 1" (2.5 cm) deep, add 3" (7.6 cm) to each end for a total overhang of 4" (10.2 cm).

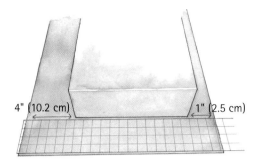

4" (10.2 cm)　　1" (2.5 cm)

Steps

1. Work with the good side of the paper facing down and the long length of the paper facing away from you. Fold the raw edge up ½" (1.3 cm) to make a nice clean edge to start with. Starting at a point that will fall ½" (1.3 cm) up from where the paper will go over the bottom of the box, fold the paper into a cone shape.

2. Fold the cone again and crease it into place with the bone folder. Turn the paper over and unfold the cones, leaving the first ½" (1.3 cm) fold in place for a clean edge.

3. Pull the first diagonal crease toward the clean edge, maintaining the angle of the fold. The fold should be ¼" (6 mm) or less.

4. Pull the second diagonal crease toward the clean edge, maintaining the angle of the fold. When pulling the second crease into place, it should form a perfect point with the first fold and the clean edge. Make sure that second fold does not become too deep at the top.

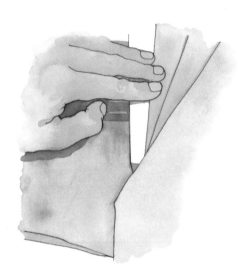

5. Use the bone folder to crease the folds into place. Turn the paper back over and tape the folds into place using long pieces of single-sided tape on the diagonal.

6. Follow steps 8 through 10 of the Three-Pleat Wrap (see page 31) to adhere the paper to the box. Finish the ends of the box just as you would with a plain wrap (see Basics, page 24). Pay special attention to where the point of the fan falls on the box. The point should always be ½" to 1" (1.3–2.5 cm) in and up on the front of the box and should never fall on the end of the box.

Follow steps 8 through 10 of the Three-Pleat Wrap (see page 31); see Basics, page 24

materials

medium-weight
　wrapping paper

single-sided tape

double-sided tape

tools

ruler

scissors

bone folder

Styling Tip

The angle of the cone should not be too severe. If the angle is too large, there will not be enough paper to cover the ends of the box.

Pleat Variations

Once you have mastered the Three-Pleat Wrap and the Tuxedo Pleat, you can build on the basic principles. Covering the entire front—or even the entire box—with pleats makes for a very impressive package. The pleats can stand alone or act as a stage for ribbons and other embellishments. Experiment with the placement of pleats on the box; try placing them to the left, to the right, or in the center. The following are a few variations on pleating, but the possibilities are endless.

Mini Pleats

Pleats and Prints

Styling Tips

This all-over effect works best on packages no larger than 10" x 10" (25.4 x 25.4 cm). It is difficult to keep the lines straight and even when covering a larger box.

Paper choice is important for this wrap. A lightweight paper is best; never use anything heavy. Also avoid shiny or waxy papers because they tend to crack at the fold lines.

It is important to use the bone folder to achieve crisp pleats. Use the bone folder on the back of the pleats before taping them down.

More pleats means more tape; be sure to use several long pieces of single-sided tape on the diagonal to hold the pleats in position.

The ends of the box will be bulky, so when closing the ends, tape the flaps into position first with single-sided tape, and then use double-sided tape to adhere the paper to the box. If the end is too bulky and will not stick, use a hot glue gun to close the ends of the box.

Styling Tips

A nice way to use Mini Pleats on a larger package is to cover only a portion of the box.

It is best to pleat a solid paper or small print. Pleating on a large print looks very busy and confusing.

To achieve this look with two papers, wrap the entire package in the dominant paper. Pleat a second paper and attach it to the box using double-sided tape along the seam of the two papers.

This layout can also be used with a fan pleat on the body of the box and Mini Pleats as a header to top off the fan.

Multiple Tuxedo Pleats

Overlapping Tuxedo Pleats

Styling Tips

This wrap sets the stage for a ribbon, big or small.

Avoid busy prints; use a solid paper or a paper with a small-scale print.

You can wrap a package with Mini Pleats, then add a wide strip with both edges folded under. This technique produces the same effect as a Tuxedo Pleat.

Styling Tips

The combination of the Mini Pleat and the Tuxedo Pleat works very well together. It can be worked with either pleat dominating the design.

You can use solid color paper alone or a solid and a print together.

Use a lightweight paper to avoid making the ends bulky.

This package was completely wrapped with a Mini Pleat first. A Tuxedo Pleat was made from the same paper and attached using double-sided tape. The ends of the Tuxedo Pleat do not go around the back of the box; they are folded under and taped to the side of the package.

Combinations

Styling Tips

This effect was achieved by wrapping the box first. Then two separate pleats were made using the reverse or wrong side of the paper. Both edges of the pleats were folded under for a clean edge. The pleats were then taped to the box using double-sided tape.

This wrap is best suited to solid color papers, which show off the complex pleating.

Simple ribbon is best; showy ribbon competes with the wrapping.

Styling Tip

To add depth and dimension to all pleating, after the box is completely wrapped, gently use your fingertips to flare the folds upward to make each pleat pop.

Wrapping with Bands of Paper

Gift wrapping with different bands of paper is great for several reasons. First, it looks fabulous to combine two different papers and get more use from a special or expensive paper, which can be cut and used on several gifts. It is also a great way to use up scraps of many different papers or to hide mistakes. For example, if you've cut your paper too short for the box, simply fill in the gap with a secondary paper.

Basic Bands

This simple method produces great results on many different levels, and the variations are endless. Using this technique, you will never again be short on paper.

Basic Techniques

Square Box Ends (page 26)

Getting Started

When choosing a base paper, it is not necessary for the paper to cover the entire box; there can be a gap or space instead of the paper overlapping. How big that gap or space is depends on how much of a secondary paper you have to work with. It is necessary for the base paper to cover at least three sides of the box with 1" (2.5 cm) of overhang on each end. The width of the secondary paper should be enough to cover the gap on the base paper plus at least 1" (2.5 cm) on each side, so that the ends can be turned under for a clean edge.

Steps

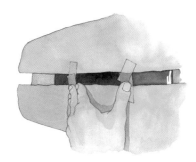

1. Often, especially with a larger square box, a single sheet of paper is too small. When this occurs, tape the base paper to the box using single-sided tape; the gap in the paper can be in the center or to the side. Close the ends of the box using the standard Square Box Ends technique. Do not worry about the gap on the top and at the ends because it will be covered by the secondary paper.

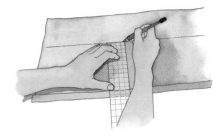

2. On the wrong side of the secondary paper, use a ruler to mark the width of the band, which will go around at least three sides of the box with some extra for folding under. Add 1" (2.5 cm) to each side so that you can turn the edges under. Mark these lines with a pencil.

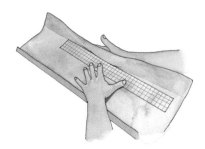

3. Using the straight edge of the ruler, fold the band on the drawn lines. Using a ruler helps keep all the folds straight, which can be difficult as the fold gets longer.

4. Make another band from the secondary paper by repeating steps 2 and 3. Attach the bands to the box using lengths of double-sided tape placed on the wrong side of the bands about ½" (1.3 cm) from the edges. To finish the bands, fold under 1" (2.5 cm) and use double-sided tape to attach them to the bottom. The bands do not cover the bottom of the box; they are simply folded under.

materials

base wrapping
    paper

secondary wrap-
    ping papers

single-sided tape

double-sided tape

tools

ruler

pencil

scissors

bone folder

Author's Advice

Do not place double-sided tape too close to the edge of the bands—it will prevent you from flaring the edge up to add emphasis and depth to the fold.

materials

base wrapping
paper

secondary
wrapping paper

single-sided tape

double-sided tape
or hot glue gun
and glue sticks

tools

ruler

pencil

craft knife

cutting mat

Striped Bands

Try using a striped wrapping paper when using the band technique. Run the stripes on the base paper in one direction and then run the stripes on the band in the other direction. This can add a lot of visual interest to an ordinary stripe. Or consider adding a third band from the base paper and laying this band on top of the second, in the same direction as the base paper. Flare the edges of the bands with your fingertips to make them pop up.

Cut Bands from Embossed Paper

The paper for this beautiful wrap is not "traditional" gift wrapping paper. It is an embossed paper from PaperMojo, a supplier that sells many gorgeous papers that are traditionally used for bookmaking. Although the paper is not heavy weight, it would be very difficult to get a clean fold. Cutting bands from heavier paper is the way to go.

Basic Techniques

Square Box Ends (page 26)

Steps

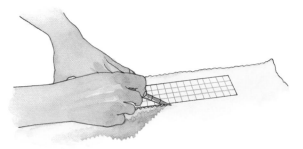

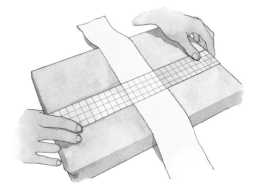

1. Tape the base paper to the box using single-sided tape; the gap in the paper can be in the center or to the side. Close the ends of the box using the standard Square Box Ends technique. Do not worry about the gap on the top and at the ends because it will be covered by the secondary paper.

2. On the wrong side of the secondary paper, use a ruler to mark the width of the bands, which will go around at least three sides of the box with some extra for folding under. Add 1" (2.5 cm) to each side so that you can turn under the edges. Mark these lines with a pencil. Use a craft knife and a cutting mat to cut the bands. (Scissors do not produce an even edge on thick paper, and precision is important.)

3. Make another band from the secondary paper by repeating step 2. Attach the bands to the box using long lengths of double-sided tape placed on the wrong side of the bands about ½" (1.3 cm) in from the edges, or use a hot glue gun for more difficult paper. To finish the bands at the bottom of the box, fold under 1" (2.5 cm) and use double-sided tape or glue to attach the bands to the bottom of the box. The bands should overlap by about ½" (1.3 cm) on the back.

Pleated Bands

The banding technique can be taken one step further by incorporating pleats into the bands. It can also save a gift wrap if there was a mistake in the original pleat.

Styling Tips

Wrap the box in a base paper and make pleats from a secondary paper. Cut the pleats from the secondary paper, fold the raw edge under, and use double-sided tape to attach the pleat to the box.

If wrapping a box using the Three-Pleat Wrap and the pleat is too short to cover the box, cut it off and make a new Tuxedo Pleat to fill the gap, using the same or contrasting paper.

CHAPTER TWO

Wrapping Odd-Shaped Items

In a perfect world, every gift would fit into a rectangular shirt box. In reality, we are most often left to wrap odd-shaped items that did not come with a box. This chapter will discuss solutions for hard-to-wrap items. No gift bags, please! Every item can be wrapped in some way or another.

Odd doesn't have to mean oddball—there are many creative solutions for wrapping oddly shaped and oversized items.

Envelope Wrap

The Envelope Wrap serves several purposes. It's a great wrap for odd-shaped items and for regular items that did not come in a box. The Envelope Wrap is also great for wrapping smaller, less valuable gifts.

Getting Started

Paper choice is important for the Envelope Wrap. Ideally, a soft paper is best, but most wrapping paper will do. It is best to avoid heavy paper or very glossy paper, which will crack when folded.

Steps

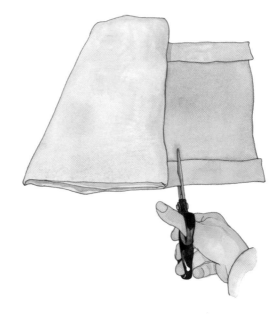

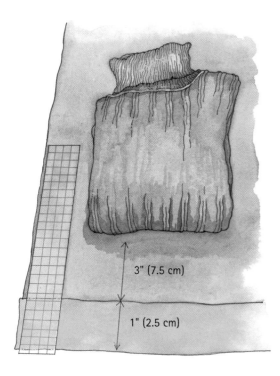

3" (7.5 cm)

1" (2.5 cm)

1. The most important step in this wrap is sizing the paper, and the depth of the item must be taken into account. If the item is 3" (7.6 cm) high, add 3" (7.6 cm) to both ends, plus 1" (2.5 cm) on each end to be folded under.

2. The length of paper needed for the wrap should go around the object approximately 1½ times.

3. After the paper is properly measured and cut, fold both sides in 1" (2.5 cm) along the entire length of paper. Tape these long folds into place with short pieces of single-sided tape placed on the diagonal.

materials

wrapping paper

single-sided tape

double-sided tape

tools

ruler

scissors

pencil

hot glue gun and
    glue sticks

bone folder

tissue paper

4. Fold the paper to form a pocket or an envelope for the gift before taping it into place; make sure the gift can fit comfortably into this pocket. It is not necessary to make a hard fold where the envelope flap begins. On the inside of the envelope, make a small mark at the fold line.

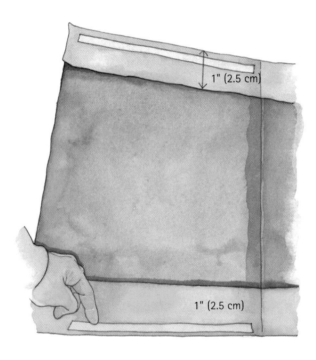

1" (2.5 cm)

1" (2.5 cm)

5. Open the paper flat again and apply one long piece of double-sided tape on each edge from the fold mark to the raw edge of the paper. Close the pocket on both sides with the double-sided tape.

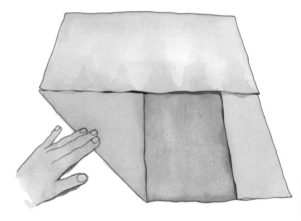

6. Use a bone folder to fold the flap into a point.

7. Depending upon what kind of gift you are wrapping, you may need to use tissue paper to fill out the corners inside before closing the envelope. Tape the flap closed or use a hot glue gun to close bulkier items.

Pleated Envelope Wrap

Just as a standard wrap can be embellished by pleats, so can the Envelope Wrap. The flap that is folded into a point on a standard envelope can easily be folded into the Three-Pleat Wrap (see page 29) or the Tuxedo Pleat (see page 32). A band of colored paper or pleated paper can also be slipped around the Envelope Wrap.

Circles

Nothing strikes fear in the heart of a gift wrapper as much as a circle. The Japanese wrap circles and tubes beautifully with the utmost precision, and I think they enjoy the challenge. Most of us wrap circular items with a soft tissuelike paper, bunching it around the item and turning it into a puffy dessert. Pleating a circular item is actually quite easy, and the finished product is very impressive.

Getting Started

Using ribbon, measure the length around the circle and add 1" (2.5 cm) for overlap. Measure the diameter of the circle on one end. The proper overhang on each end is half of the measurement of the diameter.

Steps

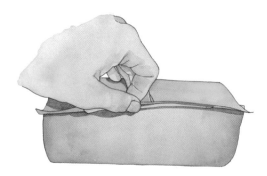

1. Using single-sided tape, attach the paper to the circle at one edge. Use a long strip of double-sided tape on the other edge to overlap and cover the circle. If the raw edge is messy, it can be folded under before taping the circle closed.

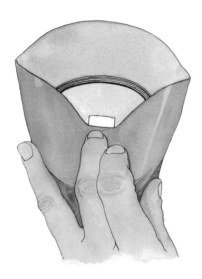

2. Work on the bottom of the circle first. Place two pieces of double-sided tape on the bottom of the box so the folds have something to adhere to. Push down the overlapping flap of paper to the edge of the box first.

3. Continue around the circle to the right, pleating at even intervals. The amount of space between the pleats will be dictated by the size of the circle and will fall into place naturally. The pleat should be very small at the edge of the circle and become larger as it falls toward the center. Each pleat will have a triangular shape.

4. Continue folding all the way around the circle. The points of the triangle will not align perfectly in the center. Repeat steps 2 and 3 for the top of the circle.

5. There are two ways to finish a circular end. You can let it stand alone and embellish it with a ribbon or flower, or you can cover the center with a small square or circle of wrapping paper.

materials

wrapping paper

single-sided tape

double-sided tape

tools

ribbon

scissors

Tubes

Tubes are usually not wrapped but are mostly adorned with a bow. What follows is a simple and traditional solution for wrapping a tube. Most versions of this technique are similar, as it is a singularly clean, stylish solution to an awkward wrapping job.

Getting Started

You'll need two pieces of paper the same size to cover the tube. The strips of paper should be as long as the tube. The width of the paper should be at least 2½ times the diameter of the tube. For example, if the tube is 2" (5.1 cm) wide, the strip of paper should be 5" (12.7 cm) wide. Use a craft knife and a cutting mat to make straight, clean cuts of paper.

Steps

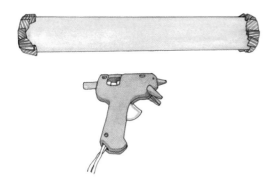

1. Trace the end of the tube onto the wrapping paper and cut around the circle with scissors about ¼" (6 mm) outside the line. Use a hot glue gun to adhere the circles to the ends of the tube.

2. Using double-sided tape, adhere two strips of paper to form a right angle. The strips should overlap to form a square in the corner where they join.

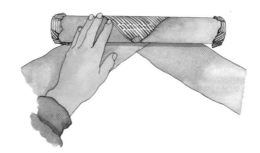

3. Using double-sided tape on the wrong side of the paper, tape the point to the center of the tube.

4. Roll the tube up into the paper, and use a few small pieces of double-sided tape to adhere the paper to the tube as you roll along.

5. Carefully trim excess paper off at the ends.

6. Adhere ribbon to both ends with a hot glue gun.

materials

wrapping paper

double-sided tape

ribbon

tools

measuring tape

craft knife

cutting mat

pencil

scissors

hot glue gun and
   glue sticks

Oversized Gifts

Often when giving a gift, it is preferable to have the gift assembled and out of the box to make a nice presentation. Examples include a child's bike at Christmas or a stroller for a baby shower. Party stores sell large gift bags for oversized items, and these are a lot like large trash bags. I prefer to wrap an item when possible, because the satisfaction of tearing the paper is always more fun than pulling an item out of a gift bag. Using this method, it is possible to wrap almost anything. Remember, big gifts demand a big bow or large embellishment.

Getting Started

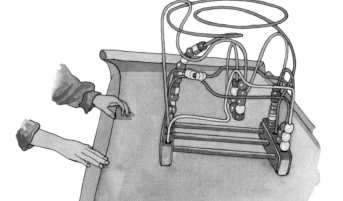

There is no magic formula for sizing paper to oversized gifts. Paper should completely go around the object in one direction. There should be enough paper at the ends so that you have an overhang where the paper meets and there is enough to fold under about 1" (2.5 cm). This method is very similar to the Envelope Wrap (see page 48) just on a larger scale.

Steps

1. Fold both long sides of paper under at least 1" (2.5 cm). These folds will form the "sides" of the box.

(see page 48)

materials

wrapping paper
 on a roll

double-sided tape

large ribbon or bow

tools

scissors

Author's Advice

If the paper is not wide enough to cover the oversized object, seam the paper together. Overlap two long lengths of paper with a 1" (2.5 cm) seam and adhere double-sided tape the entire length of the seam to hold the paper together. Instead of tape, hot glue can also be used to hold the paper together.

If the gift is very
large and awk-
ward, it may be
better to transport
the gift or place
the item under the
tree and then slip
the envelope over
it at the site of
presentation. This
is best for very
large items, such
as bicycles and
furniture.

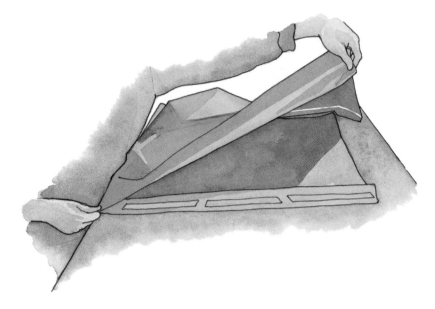

2. Fold the long length of paper in half to
form an envelope for the gift. Use long
lengths of double-sided tape the entire
length to close up the "sides" of the box.

3. With the two sides closed with double-
sided tape, slip the "envelope" over
the gift.

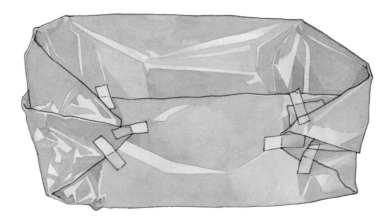

4. If the item is manageable enough to lay on its side, go ahead and close the bottom up as you would a rectangular box. It will not be a perfect end, but no one will examine the bottom of the gift.

5. Embellish the gift with a large ribbon or bow.

Think Outside the Box

This "Christmas Tree" is from the second round of the Scotch Tape Most-Gifted Wrapper contest. Please keep in mind that there was a time limit of only ten minutes. The shape of the gift, which was a large telescope, inspired the tree-style wrapping during the holiday season. Wrapping large items requires as much creativity as possible. Always try to work with the shape of the gift, and remember the gift does not have to be completely covered with paper.

CHAPTER THREE

Bow and Tie-On Techniques

As you can see by most of the wrapping in this book, the bows tend to be reserved. Most of the time, a simple elegant bow made from a beautiful ribbon is all that is needed. Many people have a very difficult time making a perfect bow. I've tutored many people on bow making, and it is the kind of thing that is very frustrating and difficult to follow. If you keep trying, one day it is like a magic door opens; you'll have mastered the perfect bow and you will never forget how to make it. A beautiful ribbon does not need a fussy bow; a simple bow can better showcase a wonderful ribbon. I could write another book on my love for ribbon. I prefer to use quality ribbons, such as satins, double-faced, hand-dyed silks, and grosgrain. Always be on the lookout for beautiful and different ribbons; yard sales, post-holiday clearance sales, and flower shops are great resources. It is wonderful to have a treasure box of carefully collected ribbons that you can call upon for a special gift wrap. A beautiful ribbon is a gift in itself, and it can be saved and used again.

Bows are as important to a gift as icing is to a cake. My philosophy on bows is that they should complement the gift wrapping, not overpower it.

Basic Bow

This basic bow technique ensures a pretty bow every time, and it is good for all ribbon types. It works especially well on single-sided ribbon, because the bow easily manipulates the ribbon to keep the good side of the ribbon facing up.

Getting Started

It is important to make sure you'll have enough length of ribbon left to form a bow after tying the ribbon around the box. To do this, make a loop with a long tail the length of which will be enough to make a bow. Place the base of the loop at the center of the box and use it as the starting point for tying the ribbon around the box.

Steps

2. After crossing the ribbon, take the long length of ribbon down around the box and back over the top.

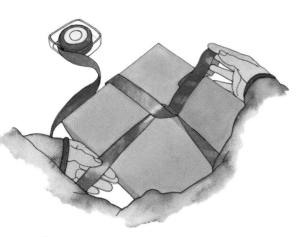

1. Take the long end of the ribbon over to the left of the box, go around the back, and come up over the right side. Cross the long end of the ribbon with the short end in the center of the box.

3. Pull the short end of the ribbon down over the long end, pull the short end under the cross in the middle, and bring it up and over to the right.

Author's Advice

Bows are rarely perfect on the first try. You'll need to make many adjustments to get the ribbon placed correctly on the box, especially if the ribbon is a precut piece instead of on a roll.

4. Pull the ribbon tight into a knot at the center of the box and form two loops of equal size for the bow.

5. Cross the left loop left over the right.

6. Push the left loop over the right one, then push the loop down and back through the hole created by the two loops.

7. Pull the left loop through the center, and then pull both loops to tighten the bow. Pull the loops and tails to adjust the shape of the bow. Cut the tails to the desired length.

Single Loop Bow

The single loop bow is very simple yet very elegant. It is a savior for those who cannot master a multiple loop bow. It's also a great bow for heavier ribbon, such as double-faced satin or velvet.

ribbon

scissors

Getting Started

The starting point for where the ribbon goes around the box needs to be as long as the desired length of the tail.

Steps

1. Cross the ribbon, bringing the short end up and over to the right.

2. Pinch a loop in the long end of the ribbon, and hold it between your thumb and first finger.

3. Bring the short end of the ribbon up and over the pinched loop.

4. Pull the short end of the ribbon through the loop.

5. Holding the loop securely, pull the short end of the ribbon to tighten the bow. Cut the tails to the desired length.

Multiple Loop Bow

The multiple loop bow has the "wow" factor—it's everything a pretty bow is supposed to be. This bow is best suited for wire-edged ribbon or sheer ribbon as it tends to get weighed down with heavier ribbon, such as double-faced satin. Once this four-loop bow is mastered, extra loops can easily be added to form a more lavish bow.

materials

ribbon

tools

scissors

Styling Tip

You can add more loops by continuing to pass ribbon over the center, forming loops on each side. The key to remember is the right-side loops should always have one less loop than the left side, because that extra loop is created in the end by pulling the short length of ribbon through the center of the bow.

Getting Started

The starting point for where the ribbon goes around the box is the same as in the Basic Bow (see page 62). Start the ribbon at the base of the pinched loop with a tail.

Steps

1. Start with the short end of the ribbon up and to the right.

2. Pinch a loop with the long end of the ribbon.

3. With the long end of the ribbon, make another loop across from the first pinched loop. Where these two loops meet will be the center of the bow. Go back across the center and, keeping all layers of ribbon pinched, form a third loop on top of the first loop.

4. Pull the short end of ribbon up and over the center of the bow. Be sure to maintain a tight pinch in the center.

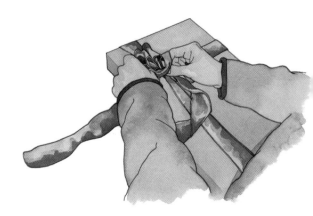

5. Continue pulling the short end of the ribbon around the center of the bow.

Ribbon Tails

To finish a bow properly, the tails of the ribbon can be cut one of two ways: on the diagonal or into a V shape. It is worth the investment to get a pair of super-sharp embroidery scissors. I find they work best for making precision cuts on better-quality ribbon.

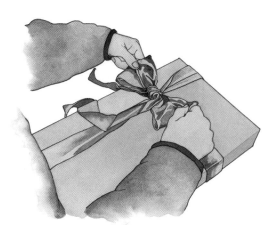

6. Maintaining a tight hold on the two left loops with your left hand, use your right hand to pull a loop of the short end of the ribbon through the center.

To make v-shaped tails, fold the ribbon in half lengthwise (it must be folded exactly in half for even tails). Using sharp scissors, cut the ribbon on a diagonal, starting the cut at the fold and cutting downward. The unfolded ribbon will have a forked tail.

7. Pull on all four loops until the center of the bow is tight. Adjust the individual loops of the bow by firmly pulling on each one.

CHAPTER FOUR

Finishing Touches

Finishing touches are those little extras that say you really put some thought into the gift. This "ooh ahh" factor can be a special ornament tied to the package or candy kisses overflowing when the package is opened. A finishing touch is most special when it is personalized to the recipient of the gift. Consider using the recipient's monogram, signature color, or favorite flower.

The layers of thoughtful detail, including gift tags and embellishments, of any wrapped gift are true finishing touches.

Embellishments

An embellishment is a great way to make a package special without a using bow and is most effective when it is something totally unexpected. Use items that are not traditionally associated with gift wrapping. Always be on the lookout for embellishments at yard sales, the dollar store, or the cake-decorating aisle of the grocery store. The scrapbooking aisle at your local craft store also offers endless possibilities for package embellishments.

More Is More!

Clustering multiples of the same or similar items makes for a truly whimsical look. Almost anything in mass can be hot glued to the top of the package, or try covering the entire box. These Christmas decorations were a yard-sale find that got a new life as a box of Christmas cheer. The mini bows came premade from a fabric store. Other suggestions that work well for this look include flowers (dried, silk, or real), miniature chocolate bars, or hard candies. It is best to use a two-piece box so the top can be removed without disturbing the items.

Fashion Forward

This simple yet elegant look is a trio of toggles made from black cording originally intended for clothing. There are many fun fashion items that can be used to embellish a gift, such as appliqués, cording, and passementerie. Of course, buttons are great to use, either glued en masse or lined up on ribbons.

Back to Nature

One of the easiest ways to embellish a gift is to walk out your front door and use whatever nature supplies.
Natural elements always complement gift wrapping.

Gift Tags

Gift tags are too important to be an afterthought. Why put a plain tag on a gift that has so much thought going into the beautiful wrapping? Just as a ribbon and an embellishment enhance the wrapping, so should a gift tag. Once again, visit the scrapbooking aisle in your craft store; there are many wonderful items that can be used as a special gift tag. Classic plain gift tags from cardstock are wonderful when they are embellished with stamps or beads. In the absence of a fabulous gift tag, attach a plain tag to the back of the package or put a note inside the box.

Ideas for Dressing Up a Package on the Inside

A perfect presentation shouldn't stop at the paper and ribbon—take care to dress up the gift on the inside as well. Adding layers to the gift adds to the suspense and uniqueness of the package. For example, people are always searching for interesting ways to present a gift certificate. Layering a gift is also important when it is a valuable or substantial present, such as an expensive piece of jewelry.

Fancy Tissue Paper

There are many decorative tissue papers on the market. Printed tissue paper or lacy cutouts inside a package can add one more element to the gift. Details on the inside of the box let the recipient know that she is truly getting something special that the giver put a lot of thought into.

Fill It Up

It's an old trick to put a smaller box inside a larger box, but it works. Nothing beats the suspense of having to open box after box to get to the prize. It is a nice idea to fill the larger box with something a little more interesting than packing peanuts. A few suggestions are flower petals (real or silk), small candies, potpourri, or the recipient's favorite cereal.

CHAPTER FIVE

Holiday Wrapping

Perhaps nothing is as fun as wrapping for holiday festivities, but for many, the pressure to perform is turned up. There never seems to be enough time. It may be a challenge to remember that wrapping can be a fun, creative project!

Combining many different papers and ribbons in unusual ways can put a welcome spin on traditional holiday wrapping. Wrapping for a holiday is a great time to slow down, to wrap thoughtfully, and to remember to embellish the sentiment behind the gift, not just the gift itself. One way to simplify holiday gift wrapping is to keep in mind the colors and themes for holidays are often universal—from the reds and greens of the winter holidays to the pastels of spring.

Holidays offer an opportunity to showcase your gift-wrapping skills and to create special wraps that will stand out from all the others.

Christmas/Boxing Day

There is Christmas wrapping when it's 11:00 P.M. on December 24th, and then there is wrapping that is as special as the gift. The most important thing to remember about holiday wrapping is not to stress out; give yourself plenty of time to be creative, and enjoy the traditions of Christmas.

Berry Christmas

The toile wrapping paper gives this package a sophisticated look and combining it with ribbons and berries make a dramatic, grown-up statement for the holiday season.

Basic Techniques

Sizing Paper to Box (page 22)

Side Seams (page 23)

Rectangular Box Ends (page 24)

Steps

1. Wrap the box using the basic techniques listed at left.

2. Tie the two ribbons as one around the box; leave the knot in the front but cut the tails short.

3. Construct the loops of the bow in two pieces and hot glue them together. Cut a short piece of ribbon to be the center of the bow and hot glue that into place as well. Hot glue the bow onto the ribbon in several places.

4. Use the hot glue gun to glue berries onto the box, and be generous with the amount of berries (test the berries with the glue gun because some artificial berries may melt under the heat of the glue gun). If you are lucky enough to have an abundance of winter berries in your yard, feel free to use them.

materials

toile wrapping paper

single-sided tape

double-sided tape

1½" (3.8 cm) -wide green ribbon with checkered border

½" (1.3 cm) -wide black and white checkered ribbon

artificial red berries

tools

ruler

pencil

scissors

bone folder

hot glue gun and glue sticks

Modern Holiday

This wrap has the sparkle of the holidays and uses geometric patterns to give it a modern edge.

materials

Christmas paper with a metallic geometric print

single-sided tape

double-sided tape

1" (2.5 cm) -wide green velvet ribbon

³⁄₈" (1 cm) -wide green satin ribbon

prewrapped mini presents (available at craft stores)

tools

ruler

pencil

scissors

bone folder

hot glue gun and glue sticks

Author's Advice

It is important to use a ruler to measure the spaces between the lines of ribbon to ensure they are all straight and even before hot gluing anything into place.

Basic Techniques

Sizing Paper to Box (page 22)

Side Seams (page 23)

Rectangular Box Ends (page 24)

Steps

1. Wrap the box using the basic techniques listed at left.

2. There are two ways to accomplish the ribbon effect on the front: the neat way or the messy way. The messy way is to tie all the ribbons off on the back of the box. Cutting the tails short still leaves a bit of a mess on the back. The neat way is to glue down all the ribbons and fold under the ends at the sides of the box. It is time-consuming, but the final result is well worth it for a special gift.

Traditional

This wrap is included because it is a wonderful example of how two different paper patterns work well together. These papers complement each other because they are in the same color family and each print is in a different scale. The papers also have a traditional, homespun Christmas look.

Basic Techniques

Sizing Paper to Box (page 22)

Rectangular Box Ends (page 24)

Tuxedo Pleat (page 32)

Steps

1. Place the large-print paper on a rectangular box with the seam on top and in the center of the box.

2. Fold a Tuxedo Pleat from the small-print paper. Fold the Tuxedo Pleat an extra two times to have two pleats on each side of the center band instead of just one.

3. Place the center band of pleats on the box using double-sided tape, and close the ends of the box.

4. Tie the ribbon in knots at the center of the package. Slip the contrasting ribbon through the loop and pull the knot tight.

Hanukkah

The choices in printed Hanukkah paper are usually pretty limited. This wrap is a festive non-traditional Hanukkah gift wrapping that still incorporates the colors and symbolism of the holiday. The lizard paper detailing is in the traditional blue color of the Israeli flag, and eight tiny bows are used to represent the eight candles on the menorah.

materials

embossed paper with lizard print
(Kate's Paperie)

single-sided tape

double-sided tape

1⅛" (2.8 cm) -wide shiny metallic silver ribbon

1" (2.5 cm) -wide blue satin ribbon

⅜" (1 cm) -wide shiny metallic silver ribbon with wire edge

tools

ruler

pencil

scissors

bone folder

ribbon scissors

hot glue gun and glue sticks

Basic Techniques

Sizing Paper to Box (page 22)

Rectangular Box Ends (page 24)

Tuxedo Pleat (page 32)

Basic Bow (page 62)

Steps

1. Wrap the box using the basic techniques listed above.

2. Place the Tuxedo Pleat in the center of the box. The embossed paper is a heavier weight, so extra care must be taken to crease the pleats firmly and crease all the sides and ends of the box. Because of the heavy paper, the ends of the box may require hot glue to keep them in place.

3. Layer the three ribbons as shown and center them on top of each other. Tie them in a knot in the back, and trim the tails of the knot short.

4. Make eight tiny bows from the wired-edge ribbon using the Basic Bow technique. Glue them onto the box in a random up, down, and sideways pattern.

Kwanzaa

The themes of the Kwanzaa holiday have many natural elements. This wrap reflects those themes by using the traditional colors of Kwanzaa—black, green, and red—and paper made from natural fibers. The softness of the netting and straw is a nice contrast to the hard edges of the green and black.

Basic Techniques

Sizing Paper to Box (page 22)

Side Seams (page 23)

Steps

1. Wrap the box in the black embossed paper using the basic techniques listed above.

2. Add a separate band of green paper. When using a thinner paper to make a decorative band, fold the paper over so the paper is doubled and meets in the center of the band. (If you only fold the band under 1" [2.5 cm] on each side, you'll be able to see through the paper and see the folded edges.)

3. Center gift on a full sheet of netting. Wrap netting around all sides of the box, gather, and tie netting in a knot at the top of the gift. Take the time to be artistic in arranging the netting. Note: Do not cut the netting, as it will fray and fall apart.

4. Tie a generous amount of raffia around the gathered netting at the top of the box.

materials

black embossed paper

single-sided tape

double-sided tape

green paper with natural fibers embedded in the paper

red netting (traditionally used in hat making, it can be found in most craft stores)

natural or synthetic raffia

tools

scissors

New Year's

In many countries, especially those in Asia, the New Year is a much bigger holiday than Christmas, and people exchange many gifts at this time. One look at this gift and its sparkle and energy says, "Happy New Year!"

Basic Techniques

Sizing Paper to Box (page 22)

Side Seams (page 23)

Rectangular or Square Box Ends (page 24 or 26)

Getting Started

This paper is very shiny and slippery, and it can be difficult to work with. I still chose to use the paper because it is so appropriate for the holiday. This paper is not suitable for pleats because it is too slick and will not hold a fold. It may be necessary to hot glue the ends closed if tape does not hold the slick paper.

Steps

1. Wrap the box in the gold paper using the basic techniques listed at left.

2. Cut a 2½" (6.4 cm) -wide band from the silver paper using a craft knife and cutting mat. The band must be cut; it cannot be folded under at the edges because they will show through the holes. Measure and mark the placement of the holes. The holes are punched in the center of the band, leaving ½" (1.3 cm) on each side of the holes. There is 1" (2.5 cm) between each hole.

3. Attach the band to the package using small pieces of double-sided tape or hot glue. Glue the trim inside the circles.

materials

shiny metallic gold paper

shiny metallic silver paper

single-sided tape

double-sided tape

wire trimmed with gold stars

tools

ruler

pencil

scissors

hot glue gun and glue sticks

craft knife

cutting mat

1½" (3.8 cm) -diameter hole punch

Saint Valentine's Day

Valentine's Day is a huge gift-giving holiday in the United States, and there are many different versions of it in countries throughout the world. Its name may vary in other countries, but the theme is universal: it is a day to give a gift to that special someone in your life. There are fun and sweet valentines and there are sexy valentines. Unique wrapping for a valentine is important because it means you took the extra time and effort to make your gift special. Letting someone know how special he is to you is the whole idea behind Valentine's Day.

materials

red velvet paper
(Kate's Paperie)

3" (7.6 cm) -wide
vintage lace

⅞" (2.2 cm) -wide
double-faced
red satin
ribbon

tools

ruler

pencil

scissors

hot glue gun
and glue sticks

bone folder

ribbon scissors

Romantic Valentine

Use red velvet and lace for a truly romantic valentine.

Basic Techniques

Sizing Paper to Box (page 22)

Side Seams (page 23)

Tuxedo Pleat (page 32)

Basic Bow (page 62)

Getting Started

Because of the heaviness and textural quality of the velvet paper, I recommend using a hot glue gun on the entire package. Be careful with the hot glue because any drips on the velvet paper will make a permanent mark.

Steps

1. Wrap the box in red velvet paper using the basic techniques listed above. Using the bone folder for crisp folds, make a separate Tuxedo Pleat.

2. Glue the lace to the box only on the edge that will be hidden under the pleat.

3. Glue the pleat to the box, folding it under at the bottom sides of the box so that the pleat does not go around to the back of the box.

4. Using the red satin ribbon, tie a Basic Bow to finish the gift.

Funny Valentine

When love is new, it is often fun; this wrap reflects that in a playful way.

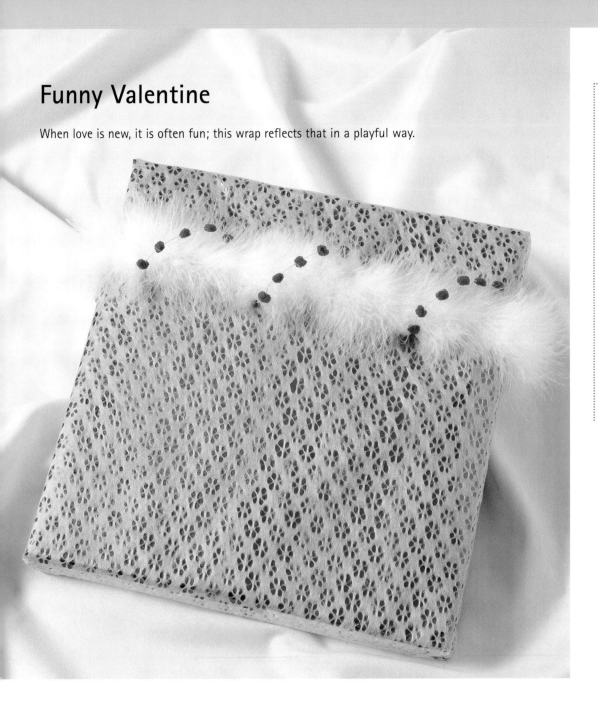

materials

red paper

pink lace flower
    paper

single-sided tape

double-sided tape

white boa

red pompom trim

tools

scissors

Basic Techniques

Sizing Paper to Box (page 22)

Side Seams (page 23)

Rectangular or Square Box Ends (page 24 or 26)

Steps

1. Wrap the box in paper using the basic techniques listed above. There are two options to use when wrapping a sheer paper over another paper. Each paper can be wrapped separately or at the same time. To wrap both papers at the same time, use several small pieces of double-sided tape to attach the sheer paper to the solid paper at the long edges that will form the side seam, then wrap, treating the two sheets of paper as one. However, I think that better results are achieved wrapping each paper separately.

2. Wind the red pompom trim loosely around the white boa. Tie the trim in a small knot in the back.

Easter

The movement in this wrap, the angle of the band, and the fluffy bow all work to convey the feeling of spring!

Basic Techniques

Sizing Paper to Box (page 22)

Side Seams (page 23)

Rectangular Box Ends (page 24)

Multiple Loop Bow (page 67)

Steps

1. This wrap begins with a basic wrap of a rectangular shirt box, following the basic techniques listed above; the interest is added with the placement of the band. Many of the wraps in this book feature the placement of the band either vertically or horizontally, but placing a band on the diagonal can add a lot of interest to a wrap.

2. Fold the edges of the band under and use double-sided tape to adhere the edges to the bottom sides of the box. (The band does go around to the back of the box.)

3. Make a Multiple Loop Bow with the sheer purple ribbon, adding extra loops.

4. Glue the purple and pink ribbons to the band along with the bow and the rabbit.

materials

pink and yellow polka dot paper

solid pink paper

single-sided tape

double-sided tape

1½" (3.8 cm) -wide sheer purple ribbon

⅞" (2.2 cm) -wide purple grosgrain ribbon

⅛" (3 mm) -wide pink ribbon with white dots

white paper rabbit

tools

ruler

pencil

scissors

bone folder

ribbon scissors

hot glue gun and glue sticks

Mother's Day

This wrap for Mother's Day is sweet and pretty; the beautiful marble paper and trim are meant to be an indulgence—something Mom would never do for herself.

Basic Techniques

Sizing Paper to Box (page 22)

Side Seams (page 23)

Basic Bow (page 62)

Steps

1. Wrap the box in marble paper using the basic techniques listed above.

2. Treating the two ribbons as one, tie them together around the box. Knot them in the back and cut the tails short.

3. Using ⅛" (3 mm) -wide ribbon, tie on the decorative letter at the center where the ribbons cross.

4. Make a separate Basic Bow from the satin ribbon and attach it using hot glue or a straight pin so as not to damage the ribbon.

materials

handmade marble
   paper (PaperMojo)

single-sided tape

double-sided tape

1⅜" (3.5 cm) -wide
   double-faced
   cream satin ribbon

¾" (1.9 cm) -wide
   vintage brocade
   ribbon

7" (17.8 cm) pearl
   monogram letter

⅛" (3 mm) -wide
   cream ribbon

tools

ruler

pencil

scissors

ribbon scissors

hot glue gun and
   glue sticks or
   straight pin

Father's Day

There are some universal sports and hobby themes for Father's Day, but it is best to pick Dad's favorite pastime and play up that theme. The masculine grosgrain ribbon balances the femininity of this fluffy bow. Finding this miniature lantern in a camping store was an inspirational moment. I should have bought more—a good embellishment is sometimes hard to find!

Basic Techniques

Sizing Paper to Box (page 22)

Side Seams (page 23)

Rectangular Box Ends (page 24)

Multiple Loop Bow (page 67)

Getting Started

It is important to keep in mind the scale of the print when wrapping. This fish print is very large and only works well because the box is big enough that you get to see a good repeat of the print. Avoid using large prints on small boxes. Also, when using such a busy print, it is a good idea to have a solid band as a backdrop for trims and bows. The solid background will help the bow pop instead of getting lost in the busy print.

Steps

1. Wrap the box following the basic techniques listed at left.

2. Create a separate decorative band from solid paper, of any dimensions desired. Place it on the box, and secure it using double-sided tape.

3. Tie lengths of solid and striped grosgrain ribbon around the decorative band, placing the knots on the back side of the gift.

4. Make a separate Multiple Loop Bow from sheer ribbon. Anchor it to the package using a separate length of striped grosgrain. Tie the lantern onto the bow using a separate length of thin ribbon.

materials

fish print paper

solid green paper

single-sided tape

double-sided tape

1½" (3.8 cm) -wide green grosgrain ribbon

⅝" (1.6 cm) -wide green striped grosgrain ribbon

1½" (3.8 cm) -wide sheer green ribbon

Coleman lantern keychain

tools

ruler

pencil

scissors

ribbon scissors

Fourth of July

This patriotic showstopper would be a wonderful hostess gift or party centerpiece, and it is perfect for those born on the Fourth of July. The best parts of this wrap are the wonderful bows. They are purchased flat, but an ingenious design detail means that by pulling a ribbon in the center you can make them nice and full. Because they are premade, they are all the exact same size; their uniformity makes them attractive to use in multiples.

Basic Techniques

Sizing Paper to Box (page 22)

Side Seams (page 23)

Rectangular Box Ends (page 24)

Steps

1. Wrap the box in blue paper using the basic techniques listed above.

2. The white and red ribbon going around the sides can be tied into a small knot on one side with the tail cut short, or it can be folded under at a corner and glued down.

3. To get the metallic trim to stand up in the middle, punch a small hole through the lid of the box and apply a small amount of hot glue to the stalks to hold them in place.

4. Glue the premade bows to the top of the package.

materials

blue paper

single-sided tape

double-sided tape

1½" (3.8 cm) -wide white ribbon

⅞" (2.2 cm) -wide red ribbon

metallic trim

red, white, and blue premade satin bows

tools

ruler

pencil

scissors

hot glue gun and glue sticks

hole punch

CHAPTER SIX

Special Occasion Wrapping

Special occasions are events other then holidays that require gift wrapping. The challenge is to create a themed gift wrap without going for the obvious printed "Happy Birthday" or "Baby Girl" paper.

Gift wraps are most successful when a gift's theme can be subtly carried through to every element of the wrap.

Birthday

Up to this point, most of the gift wraps in this book have had a more serious, grown-up style. These birthday gift wraps are themed for children. A child is not going to be appreciative of intricate folding; rather, a gift wrap for a child should be bright and bold. When wrapping for a child, make sure the gift has some kind of embellishment to catch the child's eye immediately and get her excited. She'll think, "If it looks this good on the outside, there must be something really great for me on the inside!"

Birthday Bear

Always be well stocked with interesting tie-ons and embellishments. This charming bear is not the main gift. Instead of tying the bear to the front of the box, I've created much more interest by having him pop out of the box. To create this effect, first cut a small hole in the box before wrapping it. The hole in the box should be small so that the bear is snug in place when pulling him out. After cutting the hole, put the whole bear in the box (you'll pull his head through later). After the box is completely wrapped, carefully use a craft knife to cut the paper over the hole in the box. Cut the paper in slices like a pizza; do not completely cut away the paper. Pull the bear gently through the opening, and use extra pieces of paper cut in random shapes to highlight the tear-through effect.

Truck Stop

Bows and ribbons are not just for girls, and this gift will please any little boy. It would be enough to glue little toy cars onto a gift, but the scale of this truck is what catches the eye. The ribbon completes the theme by incorporating orange and black construction colors.

Garden Party

Just one word is needed for this gift wrap—*fun*. What is it? Some people may not be sure, but one thing is certain: most people have never seen a gift wrapped quite like this. Anyone would be enchanted by it. Sometimes, ordinary objects such as these miniature paper umbrellas can have the most interesting effect when used in an unexpected way.

Hostess Gift

This handbag is the perfect wrap for a favorite girlfriend. It's a fun and whimsical wrap that can be made using the trendiest colors, papers, and ribbons. It lets the hostess know that you think of her as a stylish friend. This wrap is also good for a wedding shower or a party favor, and it could be done using the Envelope Wrap (see page 48) instead of using a box and have a soft "purse."

Basic Techniques

Sizing Paper to Box (page 22)

Rectangular Box Ends (page 24)

Basic Bow (page 62)

Getting Started

Keep in mind the shape of the box when doing this wrap. Rectangular boxes work best because square handbags are simply not as common.

Steps

1. Wrap the box using standard Rectangular Box Ends, but have the ends on the long sides of the box. Doing this keeps the folded end covered by the flap and the short sides clean for a much neater look.

2. Make a "purse strap" by folding a strip of paper three times; the strap should be as wide as the side of the box. Using a hot glue gun, glue florist wire onto the two sides of the strap and glue the strap closed. Glue the strap to one of the long sides of the box.

3. Make a flap to cover the top of the box and part of the front. When making the flap, the paper should be folded over and doubled. All four sides of the flap should be folded under for a clean edge.

4. Embellishing this "handbag" wrap is half the fun. In addition to ribbon, items such as flowers, pins, or a scarf could also be used.

materials

polka dot wrapping paper *(Midori)*

single-sided tape

double-sided tape

$\frac{5}{8}$" (1.6 cm) -wide grosgrain ribbon

$\frac{1}{4}$" (6 mm) -wide satin ribbon

tools

ruler

pencil

scissors

hot glue gun and glue sticks

florist wire

bone folder

Graduation

This wrap shows a sophisticated use of multiple Tuxedo Pleats. Remember that pleats in all sizes and of different papers can be made separately and attached to a basic wrap. The marble paper in a sophisticated color adds to the graduation theme, but this wrap could also be done using any school colors. The embellishments add the final touch for the theme.

Basic Techniques

Sizing Paper to Box (page 22)

Side Seams (page 23)

Rectangular Box Ends (page 24)

Tuxedo Pleat (page 32)

Basic Bow (page 62)

Steps

1. Wrap the box in marble paper using the basic techniques listed at left. The box can be wrapped with a side seam, or the paper can be seamed under one of the Tuxedo Pleats.

2. Make three separate Tuxedo Pleats exactly the same size. Attach the pleats to the box with double-sided tape. The pleats will not go around to the back of the box. Fold the pleats under at the bottom edge of the sides of the box and tape them in place.

3. Using a computer, print out the word *Congratulations* to the proper scale for the size of the gift. Roll up a plain piece of paper into a tube to provide stability, and then wrap the printed paper around the previously made roll.

4. Glue the paper to the box and trim with the ribbon and tassel.

materials

handmade marble
    paper *(PaperMojo)*

single-sided tape

double-sided tape

plain paper

¼" (6 mm) -wide
    black satin ribbon

3" (7.6 cm) gold tassel

tools

ruler

pencil

scissors

computer and printer

bone folder

hot glue gun and
    glue sticks

Wedding Shower

This wrap is the Envelope Wrap all dressed up with a decorative Pleated Band, and the gold paper and ribbon add a special touch. Often, for bridal and baby showers, odd-shaped items need to be wrapped. The Envelope Wrap is a perfect solution for hard-to-wrap gifts.

Basic Techniques

Pleated Bands (page 45)

Envelope Wrap (page 48)

Multiple Loop Bow (page 67)

Steps

1. Make a basic Envelope Wrap from the printed paper.

2. Make a decorative Pleated Band from the gold crinkled paper. The band will not go around to the back of the envelope; the ends will be folded under at the seams. Because of the texture and metallic finish of both papers, the band should be attached to the envelope using hot glue; regular tape will not hold the two metallic papers together.

3. Make two separate Multiple Loop Bows with each of the ribbons, and attach them to each other using the needle and thread. Use the needle and thread to attach the cording to the bow. Be sure to tie the ends of the cording into a knot to prevent fraying.

4. Attach the bow to the envelope using hot glue.

materials

gold print unryu paper with ribbon and leaves

gold crinkled metallic paper

double-sided tape

1¼" (3.1 cm) -wide sheer gold ribbon

⅝" (1.6 cm) -wide sheer white ribbon with gold edge

¼" (6 mm) -wide gold cording

tools

ruler

pencil

scissors

hot glue gun and glue sticks

ribbon scissors

needle and thread

Wedding

Weddings are an opportunity to do an elegant and dramatic gift wrapping. White goes beautifully with silver and gold, and stacking boxes creates a grand effect that is always perfect for a wedding. This tiered wrap works well for gifts such as a towel set or a china place setting. It's a very easy wrap to do, but it just takes a little more time to wrap four boxes instead of one.

Basic Techniques

Sizing Paper to Box (page 22)

Rectangular Box Ends (page 24)

Basic Bow (page 62)

Steps

1. Wrap each box separately following the basic techniques listed at left.

2. When stacking boxes, it is important that the bottoms of the boxes are flat. To achieve this, do not tie ribbon around the boxes; instead, adhere the ribbon to the bottoms of the boxes with a hot glue gun to eliminate bulky knots. For neatness, the ribbon on the base box can be neatly glued on top of the box because it will be covered by the second box. Use a ruler to measure the ribbon and box widths to get the ribbon centered exactly on each box. The simple elegance of this tiered wrap is that the ribbons line up precisely.

3. Use a ruler to measure each Basic Bow to make sure they are the same size. Place the bows on at least two sides or all four sides of the "cake."

materials

2 different printed papers on white background

embossed metallic paper

single-sided tape

double-sided tape

1½" (3.8 cm) -wide double-sided white satin ribbon

tools

ruler

pencil

scissors

bone folder

ribbon scissors

hot glue gun and glue sticks

Bar/Bat Mitzvah

The design and texture of this paper gives this wrap a modern look. The interest in this gift wrap is that the separate Tuxedo Pleat is used almost as a ribbon to tie the two boxes together. The contrasting styles and textures of the ribbon add more depth and interest to the wrap.

Basic Techniques

Sizing Paper to Box (page 22)

Side Seams (page 23)

Rectangular Box Ends (page 24)

Tuxedo Pleat (page 32)

Basic Bow (page 62)

Multiple Loop Bow (page 67)

Steps

1. Wrap the two boxes separately following the basic techniques listed at left, then attach them to each other with double-sided tape or hot glue.

2. Make a separate Tuxedo Pleat, adding an extra pleat to each side. The pleat can go all the way around both boxes or it can be folded under at the edges of the boxes.

3. Make a Basic Bow from the 1" (2.5 cm) grosgrain ribbon.

4. Make a separate Multiple Loop Bow from the blue sheer ribbon.

5. Attach the sheer bow to the gift using the 1/8" (3 mm) satin tied through the wide bow.

materials

wrapping paper

single-sided tape

double-sided tape

1" (2.5 cm) silver grosgrain ribbon

1/2" (1.3 cm) blue sheer wired-edge ribbon

1/8" (3 mm) blue double-faced satin ribbon

tools

ruler

pencil

scissors

bone folder

ribbon scissors

hot glue gun and glue sticks

Baby Shower

This wrap is an example of experimenting with different sizes and shapes of boxes to create an attractive look. Boxes don't always have to be stacked on top of each other in descending order. A very interesting arrangement can be from smaller to larger. Here, that one special embellishment sets the theme of the gift. The paper doesn't scream "baby shower," but the baby booties do!

Basic Techniques

Sizing Paper to Box (page 22)

Side Seams (page 23)

Square Box Ends (page 26)

Multiple Loop Bow (page 67)

Steps

1. Wrap the three boxes separately following the basic techniques listed at left, and attach them together using generous amounts of double-sided tape or hot glue.

2. Layer the solid pink, pink gingham, and sheer green ribbon, treating them as one ribbon. Tie them in a knot at the top of the package.

3. Create a separate Multiple Loop Bow from the sheer green ribbon. Attach the bow to the package using thin pink ribbon.

4. Trim all ribbon tails to an array of shorter lengths to give the embellishment a lively effect. Using hot glue, affix premade gingham bows to the gift.

materials

sweet pea paper
   (Midori)

single-sided tape

double-sided tape

1½" (3.8 cm) -wide
   pink satin ribbon

⅞" (2.2 cm) -wide
   pink gingham
   ribbon

⅝" (1.6 cm) -wide
   sheer green ribbon

⅛" (3 mm) -wide
   pink satin ribbon
   with white polka
   dots

1¼" (3.1 cm) -wide
   premade pink
   gingham bows

tools

ruler

pencil

scissors

hot glue gun and
   glue sticks

ribbon scissors

Christening

Sometimes it's good to go over the top. This wrap really celebrates a baby; it is delicate and charming and, yes, a bit extravagant, with lots of trim. Even though this wrap is very busy, it works well because the trim and paper are all one color. Remember, too much of a good thing can be delightful!

Basic Techniques

Sizing Paper to Box (page 22)

Side Seams (page 23)

Rectangular Box Ends (page 24)

Square Box Ends (page 26)

Multiple Loop Bow (page 67)

Steps

1. Wrap one square and one rectangular box in different papers following the basic techniques listed at left. Attach the boxes to each other with double-sided tape or hot glue.

2. Double the tulle, wrap it around both boxes, and tie it in a knot on top. Trim the tulle short enough to keep it perky and standing up.

3. Tie the satin-edged ribbon into a Multiple Loop Bow and push an extra length of ribbon through the base of the bow to create an extra curl on each side. Glue the bow on top.

4. To finish the package and add that extra delicate baby feel, randomly glue the mini white pompoms throughout the ribbon and tulle.

materials

white embossed paper

white polka dot paper

single-sided tape

double-sided tape

6" (15.2 cm) -wide roll of white tulle

1½" (3.8 cm) -wide sheer white ribbon with satin edge

¼" (6 mm) -wide white pompoms

tools

ruler

pencil

scissors

hot glue gun and glue sticks

ribbon scissors

Housewarming

The bee-themed paper is what makes this wrap the perfect housewarming gift. Bees are a symbol of prosperity, so they make for a warm welcome to a new house. The D-ring ribbon ties make a stylish statement and are currently a popular trend.

materials

bee-themed paper
(Midori)

single-sided tape

double-sided tape

1½" (3.8 cm) -wide
green polka dot
grosgrain ribbon

1½" (3.8 cm) -wide
sheer green ribbon

four 1¼" (3.1 cm)
-diameter D-rings

artificial flower

tools

ruler

pencil

scissors

bone folder

ribbon scissors

needle and thread
or hot glue gun
and glue sticks

Basic Techniques

Sizing Paper to Box (page 22)

Side Seams (page 23)

Square Box Ends (page 26)

Steps

1. Wrap the box using the basic techniques listed at left.

2. Layer the two ribbons together and treat as one.

3. Attach the ribbon to the D-rings with needle and thread or hot glue. Thread the ribbon through the D-rings and tighten it around the box just as you would a belt. Each ribbon should ring the package about one-third of the way from each end of the package.

4. Using hot glue, affix the flower to the package where desired.

Party Favors and Parting Gifts

Don't be tempted to grab a gift bag for small party favors. Here are two simple solutions for small party favors that don't compromise style for convenience.

Mini Envelope Wraps

Mini Envelope Wraps are perfect for small, awkward items. Cookies and chocolates can be wrapped up like little treasures in papers to coordinate with any party theme.

Slip-On Decorative Band

During the holiday season, boxes of chocolates are often sold with an added seasonal decorative band. It is very easy to incorporate this idea at home using the Tuxedo Pleat (see page 32) as a band, with paper and ribbon to match your own theme or party.

Seasonal Wraps

When giving a gift that is not for a specific holiday or event, following a seasonal theme is a thoughtful option. Use the natural and traditional colors and textures of the seasons for coordinated, aesthetically pleasing gift wrap.

Spring

This spring wrap is an example of using Mini Pleats as a separate element, and the technique works best with a natural-fiber paper. Making the pleats separately and playing up the raw edge gives this gift wrap an organic feel. The colors also reflect the spring theme.

Basic Techniques

Sizing Paper to Box (page 22)

Side Seams (page 23)

Rectangular Box Ends (page 24)

Mini Pleats (page 38)

Steps

1. Wrap the box following the basic techniques listed above.

2. For the Mini Pleats, start with a sheet of paper twice the length of the box. Before pleating it, gently tear both edges in an uneven manner. Fold the entire paper into pleats and use the bone folder for every fold because the natural fibers tend to resist a crease. Use generous amounts of single-sided tape to hold the pleats in place. Use double-sided tape or hot glue to attach the pleats to the box.

3. To make the bow, loop the ribbon back and forth on a flat surface, decreasing the loop size with each layer. Loop the tail of the ribbon back around in the opposite direction to form the center of the bow, and then secure the bow with a needle and thread.

4. Glue the bow to the box.

Summer

Nothing says summer like red gingham and strawberries. The play of the printed and solid papers creates the abstract effect of a strawberry. The solid green also serves as a background to make the ribbons pop.

materials

strawberry print
    paper

solid green paper

single-sided tape

double-sided tape

1⅜" (3.5 cm) -wide
    red and white
    gingham wire-
    edged ribbon

⅜" (1 cm) -wide
    green satin
    ribbon

tools

ruler

pencil

scissors

ribbon scissors

hot glue gun and
    glue sticks

Basic Techniques

Sizing Paper to Box (page 22)

Rectangular Box Ends (page 24)

Multiple Loop Bow (page 67)

Steps

1. Using a ruler and pencil, draw a level line around one-third of the box so you can align the papers correctly. Attach the strawberry print paper to the box with single-sided tape, covering two-thirds of the front and back.

2. Using double-sided tape, attach the solid green paper to the remaining third of the box. Attach both papers to the ends of the box at the same time, treating them as if they were one piece of paper.

3. Tie bands of green satin and gingham ribbon around the box, and then cut the tails short.

4. Make a Multiple Loop Bow with green satin and gingham ribbon and glue it to the box.

materials

paper with decorative embroidery and tassels

single-sided tape

double-sided tape

1½" (3.8 cm) -wide green satin ribbon

1" (2.5 cm) -wide gold grosgrain ribbon

½" (1.3 cm) -wide metallic gold wire-edged ribbon

chopsticks

tools

ruler

pencil

scissors

hot glue gun and glue sticks

Fall

Nothing but a fabulous wrap could come from this beautiful Asian-inspired paper. Gluing a pair of chopsticks to the edge continues the Asian theme.

Basic Techniques

Sizing Paper to Box (page 22)

Side Seams (page 23)

Rectangular Box Ends (page 24)

Getting Started

Carefully consider the paper placement on the box when working with a design that is so spread out. It would be easy to end up with no tassels on the front and four on the back. Always consider where the pattern of the paper will fall on the box before you start wrapping.

Steps

1. Wrap the box using the basic techniques listed at left.

2. Treating the green satin and gold ribbons as one, tie them around box. Place knot on the back of the gift.

3. Trim the tails of the ribbons short, adding texture to the presentation.

4. Hot glue two chopsticks together, and wrap the gold ribbon loosely around the chopsticks. Using hot glue, affix the chopsticks to the package.

Winter

Decorative hole punches (available at craft stores) are a great way to add interest to a plain paper. Hole punches are no longer just round. There are many different hole punches that will match any theme or holiday, and a hole-punched band is a great alternative for those who are bow-challenged. The simple beauty of the paper inspired the embellishment.

materials

pine print paper
(Midori)

white paper

single-sided tape

double-sided tape

tools

ruler

pencil

scissors

bone folder

craft knife

cutting mat

³⁄₄" (1.9 cm) -diameter
   snowflake hole
   punch

Basic Techniques

Sizing Paper to Box (page 22)

Tuxedo Pleat (page 32)

Steps

1. Wrap the box with pine print paper following the basic techniques listed above.

2. Center the Tuxedo Pleat on the box. The tuxedo pleat is not separate; it is folded along the right edge of the paper.

3. Cut a strip of white paper 1" (2.5 cm) wide using a craft knife and a cutting mat. Use a ruler to mark the center of the paper where the snowflake holes will go.

4. Using small pieces of double-sided tape, attach the snowflake strip to the center of the tuxedo pleat.

Teacher's Gift

This wrap demonstrates how bands can add interest to the most ordinary paper. For a school-teacher theme, I used simple construction paper but dressed it up with decorative-edge scissors. The theme is followed through using primary colors and crayons for embellishment.

Basic Techniques

Sizing Paper to Box (page 22)

Rectangular Box Ends (page 24)

Wrapping with Bands of Paper (page 41)

Multiple Loop Bow (page 67)

Steps

1. Wrap the box with construction paper following the basic techniques listed at left. Because the construction paper is so small, I used two pieces of blue to cover the box, and the overlapping bands of paper will later cover the seam.

2. Cut bands of paper using the decorative-edge scissors, and attach them to the box with double-sided tape. Fold the bands under at the bottom of the sides of the box.

3. Make a Multiple Loop Bow with the ribbon, then run an extra length of ribbon through the base of the bow to create two extra tails.

4. Carefully attach the crayons to the extra ribbon tails with hot glue, and then glue the bow to the box.

materials

4 different colors of construction paper

single-sided tape

double-sided tape

2" (5.1 cm) -wide red sheer ribbon

crayons

tools

ruler

pencil

scissors

bone folder

decorative-edge scissors

ribbon scissors

hot glue gun and glue sticks

Resources

The following companies are excellent sources for all your gift-wrapping supplies as well as decorative papers and other embellishments for presentations.

A.C. Moore
www.acmoore.com

A.I. Friedman
44 West 18th Street
New York, New York 10011 USA
212-243-9000
Calligraphy, art supplies, books, stationery items, fine papers, ribbon, frames, mat board

Aussie Scrapbook Suppliers
About.com
www.scrapbooking.about.com

Black Ink
5 Brattle Street, Harvard Square
Cambridge, Massachusetts 02138 USA
617-497-1221
and
101 Charles Street
Boston, Massachusetts 02114 USA
617-723-3883

Black Ink@Home
370 Broadway
Cambridge, Massachusetts 02139 USA
617-576-0707
Black Ink, and its spin-off of larger goods, ceramics, and furniture called Black Ink@ Home, is a treasure trove of inspiring and useful items. From ingenious "sushi-pops" to lunch boxes and bowling-ball patches, these stores cull from what's out there—kitschy, industrial, and elegant—for customers who outfit their homes and projects with their goodies.

C & J Specialty Papers, INC.
1357 A. Paz corner Apacible Street
Paco, Manila Philippines
632-561-3756 or 632-561-3791
cjsp@pacific.net.ph
www.cnjpaper.com

Charles Ro Supply Co.
662 Cross Street
Malden, Massachusetts 02148 USA
781-321-0090
www.charlesro.com

Franca Xenia
Bedfordview 2008 South Africa
+27 1 974 8464
www.paperworld.co.za

HERMA GmbH
Ulmer Strasse 300
D-70327
Stuttgart, Germany
+49 (0) 711 7902 0

HobbyCraft
Head Office
Bournemouth UK
+44 1202 596 100
Stores throughout the UK

John Lewis
Flagship Store
Oxford
London W1A 1EX UK
+44 11 20 7269 7711
Stores throughout the UK

Kanban Card and Paper
Unit 1, Jubilee Court
Bradford Yorkshire BD18 IQF UK
+44 1274 582 415

Kate's Paperie
www.katespaperie.com
Several locations:

561 Broadway
(between Prince and Spring Streets)
New York, New York 10012 USA
212-941-9816

8 West 13th Street
(between 5th and 6th Avenues)
New York, New York 10011 USA
212-633-0570

1282 Third Avenue
(at 74th Street)
New York, New York 10021 USA
212-396-3670

140 West 57th Street
(between 6th and 7th Avenues)
New York, New York 10019 USA
212-459-0700
800-809-9880

125 Greenwich Avenue
Greenwich, Connecticut 06830 USA
203-861-0025

Lazy Daisy
2 Lincoln Place
Madison, New Jersey 07990 USA
973-593-6826

Michael's Arts & Crafts
www.michaels.com
Nationwide locations

Midori
708 6th Avenue North
Seattle, Washington 98109 USA
800-659-3049
www.midoriribbon.com

New York Central Art Supply
62 Third Avenue
New York, New York 10003 USA
212-473-7705 or 800-950-6111
sales@nycentralart.com
www.nycentralart.com
Calligraphy, art supplies, books, stationery items, fine papers, frames, mat board

Paper Access
23 West 18th Street
New York, New York 10011 USA
212-463-7035 or 800-727-3701
www.paperaccess.com
info@paperaccess.net
Fine papers, stationery and mailing supplies, ribbon, rubber stamp and embossing supplies, pressed flowers

Paper & Ink Arts
3 North Second Street
Woodsboro, Maryland 21798 USA
800-736-7772 or 301-898-7991
www.paperinkarts.com or
www.paperinkbooks.com
paperinkarts@aol.com or
paperinkbk@aol.com
Calligraphy and art supplies and books, fine papers

PaperMojo
1233 Bristol Road
Churchville, Pennsylvania 18966 USA
800-420-3818
www.papermojo.com

Paper Pedlar
681 Morris Turnpike
Springfield, New Jersey 07081 USA
973-376-3385

Paper Source
www.paper-source.com
Locations include Chicago, Cambridge, Minneapolis, and Kansas City (check the website for other cities). Here you'll find papers of all kinds, both luxurious and simple. You'll also find adhesives, book-binding materials, decorations, and other high-quality goods.

Pebbles Inc.
801-235-1520
www.pebblesinc.com
wholesale paper

Pearl Paint
308 Canal Street
New York, New York 10013 USA
212-431-7932 or 800-221-6845 x2297
www.pearlpaint.com
Calligraphy, art supplies, books, fine papers, pressed flowers, rubber stamp and embossing supplies, frames, mat board

Personal Impressions
Curzon Road
Sudbury Suffolk COIO 2XW UK
+44 1787 375 241
www.richstamp.co.uk

Primrose Paperworks Co-op Art & Craft Centre
Matora Lane
Cremorne 2090
Sydney, NSW Australia
www.primrose-park.com.au
primrosepaperworks@ihug.com.au

Quill
Level 3, Power Plant Mall
Rockwell Center
Amapola corner Estrella Streets
Pl-1200 Makati City Philippines
632-898-1433
quill@lietz.com

Relma
3 Rue des Poitevins
75006 Paris, France
+33 01 43 25 40 52
relma@wanadoo.fr

Rougier et Ple
13-15 Blvd. des Filles du Calvarie
75003 Paris, France
(01) 42 72 82 90 or 0825 160 560
commandes@artacrea.fr

Sam Flax
12 West 20th Street
New York, New York 10011 USA
212-620-3038 or 800-726-3529
www.samflax.com
Calligraphy, art supplies, books, stationery items, fine papers, frames, mat board

Scotch
888-3M HELPS
www.3m.com

Treasure Island
800-648-0109
www.treasureislandstores.com
New Jersey and New York Locations

Wild Things
14 Prospect Street
Madison, New Jersey 07940 USA
973-966-9191

Acknowledgments

A big thank you to Kate's Paperie for their support and contribution of materials to the book. I'd especially like to thank Melanie for her constant encouragement with all my wrapping endeavors. Kate's is a necessary pilgrimage for all paper lovers when in New York, but if you can't make it to the city, their website (see Resources, page 124) also has a wide selection of all things paper.

I would like to thank PaperMojo for supplying all the handmade marble papers for the book. They are a wonderful online resource for decorative paper.

Also, I would like to thank Midori for supplying many of the ribbons and papers for the book. Please check their website to find store locations.

Thank you to all the wonderful people at 3M and Hunter PR who made winning the Most-Gifted Wrapper Contest a fun, exciting, and pleasant experience.

Recommended Reading

There are surprisingly few books on Japanese-style gift wrapping and paper arts that are not written in Kanji. Here are two of the best English-language volumes.

Baskett, Mickey. *Creative Paper Folding.* New York: Sterling Publishing Co., Inc, 2001.

Ekiguchi, Kunio. *Gift Wrapping: Creative Ideas from Japan.* Tokyo: Kondansha International, 1985.

About the Author

Gift-wrap stylist Christine Fritsch holds the honor of having been named Scotch Tape's Most-Gifted Wrapper of 2002. She trained in Japan—where presentation is supremely important—and has worked at premier wrapping stores such as Kate's Paperie in New York City and for private clients. She has appeared on numerous national television shows dispensing her gift-wrapping tips and has also contributed her ideas to several magazines, including *Women's Day*. She lives in Madison, New Jersey, with her husband, James, and their two sons, Wyatt and Owen.